Dodeka

Fulfilling The Great Commission By Training Disciples To
Be Fruitful And Effective Leaders

By Dr. Timothy C. Kernan

Dodeka: Fulfilling The Great Commission By Training Disciples To Be Fruitful And Effective Leaders

Copyright © 2021 by Tim Kernan

All rights reserved. No part of this publication may be reproduced, distributed, or transmitted in any form or by any means - including photocopying, recording, or other electronic and mechanical methods - without the prior written permission of the author (except in the case of brief quotations embodied in critical reviews, sermons, lessons, articles, and certain other non-commercial uses permitted by copyright and fair usage law). For permission requests, please email the author at the address below:

Tim Kernan: tim@usd21.org

Updated July 4, 2021

SoldOut Press International
Editor-in-Chief - Dr. Kip McKean

ISBN-13: 978-1724344021
ISBN-10: 1724344021

Table Of Contents

Acknowledgments 6

Foreword 7

Dodeka 9

    Suggested Resource List 13

    Memory Scriptures 13

    Preface: Selection Of Your Dodeka 14

    Study 1: Quiet Times 17

    Study 2: Personal Evangelism Skills 20

    Study 3: Conversion Study Skills 23

    Study 4: Counting The Cost Skills 29

    Study 5: Discipling Skills 33

    Study 6: Bible Talk Leadership Skills 37

    Study 7: The Teen Ministry 42

    Study 8: The Campus Ministry 46

    Study 9: The Marrieds / Singles Ministry 50

    Study 10: Shepherding Skills 53

    Study 11: Fund Raising Skills 57

    Study 12: Restoration Skills 61

Epilogue 64

Acknowledgments

First and foremost, I am so grateful to God for the incredible honor of being a disciple and serving as an Evangelist in His Kingdom. To be empowered and entrusted to impact people with the Gospel is a beautiful blessing and sobering responsibility.

Thank you to my lovely wife, Lianne, who has been a constant encouragement and friend for so many years. You become more beautiful and spiritual every year.

Thank you to my amazing children, Tim Jr. and David. You are a joy to come home to every day! I am so grateful for the men you are becoming!

An immense thank you to Kip and Elena McKean for being a father and mother in the faith to Lianne and me. Thank you for your unswerving focus on seeking and saving the lost, as well as insisting that I be the same way.

Thank you as well to the Causeys, Challinors, Dimitrys, Underhills, Carrs, Bakers, Gregorys, McDonnells, McGees, Hardings, Keenans, Kirchners, Bordieris, Olmoses, Untalans, and everyone else who does such a great job serving and propelling the Tribe Pacific Rim World Sector and the SoldOut Movement forward. Thank you for your single-minded focus on making our church a mission-oriented, loving, and Godly fellowship.

Thank you to every member of the City of Angels International Christian Church - past and present. You are the tip of the spear.

Foreword

"Ezra was up on the high platform, where he could be seen by everyone, and when he opened the book, they all stood up. Ezra praised the great Lord God, and the people shouted, "Amen! Amen!" Then they bowed with their faces to the ground and worshiped the Lord. After this, the Levites... went among the people, explaining the meaning of what Ezra had read. The people started crying when God's Law was read to them." (Nehemiah 8: 1-8)

It is an honor to write the forward for Dr. Tim Kernan's new book *Dodeka!* I have had the privilege of working with and learning from Tim in Orange County, California, for the last two years. During this time, Tim has mentored me, taught me priceless life principles, and unlocked much of the "inner leader" in me through God's Word and his leadership. In these two years, we have seen over 100 strong Christians sent to the mission field from our ministry in Orange County and were still blessed with over 20% growth in the last year.

It is to God's glory to see a ministry become a leadership fountain that fuels world evangelism. I have realized this is not such an easy task, even for those with the greatest intentions. We need faith, biblical principles, and practicals to be taught and applied in order to train leaders and send them out at a radical pace. *Dodeka* is the brass tacks - the simple, effective leader-making book you have been looking for to take your ministry to the next level.

In *Dodeka,* Tim has identified vital leadership areas and extracted relevant Scriptures to enhance any Christian's basic leadership skill set. *Dodeka* draws you toward God and teaches you how to grasp these Godly principles to propel your walk and make a great impact.

I urge you to study *Dodeka* for yourself and then take anyone you mentor through it. This is also an excellent ministry book and an enlightening series for your church or small group. Prepare to see a dramatic change in your ministry from the minute you pick up *Dodeka* and begin to apply these timeless principles.

Brian Carr
Revolution Super Region Leader
City Of Angels International Christian Church

April 30, 2021

Then Jesus came to them and said, "All authority in heaven and on earth has been given to me. Therefore go and make disciples of all nations, baptizing them in the name of the Father and of the Son and of the Holy Spirit, and teaching them to obey everything I have commanded you. And surely I am with you always, to the very end of the age." (Matthew 28:18-20)

Welcome to the *"Dodeka Series!"* "Dodeka" is the Greek word for "Twelve." Jesus selected and trained a small group of twelve *"unschooled and ordinary men"* as He called them to imitate His example. (Acts 4:13) Teaching them to be fruitful and effective, they became powerful leaders who would turn the world upside down at the cost of their lives.

For Jesus, raising up the Dodeka was of supreme importance for the fate of humanity hung on two factors: His willingness to die on the cross and the ability of His Dodeka to proclaim the Gospel to a dark and lonely world effectively. The same is true for us today.

As leaders in God's Kingdom, we must imitate Jesus and raise our own Dodeka. Ron Harding recently reminded me of something Kip McKean said in the earliest days of the Movement: "When you get your church to 100, we see what God has done through you. When you get your church over

100, then we see what God has done through your few." Historically, so many churches in the Restoration Movement stagnate at about 100 members or less because that is all that the primary leader can sustain alone.

In other words, ministries without a Dodeka get to a seemingly impenetrable ceiling of about 100 members and then "meltdown" to about 70 in a painful and faith stealing cycle. However, in the SoldOut Movement, we believe that every church leader should be training a powerful Dodeka. From scratch, they are taught to be fruitful Bible Talk and House Church Leaders that God can use to take a church into the hundreds and beyond.

> *When He saw the crowds, He had compassion on them, because they were harassed and helpless, like sheep without a shepherd. Then He said to His disciples, "The harvest is plentiful but the workers are few. Ask the Lord of the harvest, therefore, to send out workers into His harvest field.* (Matthew 9:36-39)

This was Jesus' mindset. At the end of the day, it is the final word on evangelism. *"The harvest is plentiful but the workers are few. Ask the Lord of the harvest, therefore, to send out workers into His harvest field."* When there is little harvest, few are praying to be workers and to make workers! We must be utterly unyielding in this perspective. *Dodeka* seeks to help you raise up your own "twelve" who will become true "workers for the Lord!" The result will be an abundant harvest!

Just as the First Principles guide the lost through the Biblical teaching necessary to be ready for baptism, the *Dodeka Bible*

Study Series aims to train and prepare disciples to be equipped for leadership.

To put it another way, one of the outstanding elements of the Restoration Movement is our "oral tradition." This refers to the collection of treasured Bible insights that have been mined from the Scriptures and passed down verbally from teacher to student. Even concepts like "evangelism," "discipling" and "quiet times," are part of this verbally shared biblical knowledge. This Bible Study Series is an effort to capture this vocally transmitted basic leadership teaching to paper. With it, we can patiently and carefully raise up large numbers of leaders with confidence.

Therefore, *Dodeka* is an intermediate step but an essential one between the freshly baptized disciple and a Bible Talk Leader, an ICCM student, or another leadership role in the Kingdom. By spending time together, reading these Scriptures, sharing your insights as the study guides you, and putting them into practice, you will build great relationships and rock-solid leadership convictions.

By applying the Scriptures highlighted in this series, you can build a team that will be the "tip of the spear," "where the rubber meets the road," and at the "cutting edge" of Jesus' mission. After each study, expect tangible change from those with whom you are studying and "make" a leader as you progress through this series.

I taught these same studies to my Dodeka, and I challenged them to teach them to theirs. So, in essence, this book is for church leaders, region leaders, and interns to be trained and to train others for leadership.

The main question now is: With whom are you going to do these studies?

Your brother,
Tim

April 30, 2021

Suggested Resource List

Elevate - Jesus' Global Revolution For Women: Dr. Elena McKean
Money Is The Answer For Everything: Joe Willis
Paper Tigers - A Christian Woman's Guide To Overcoming: Dr. Lianne S. Kernan
Proven Genuine - An Examination Of Suffering In The Book Of Job: Dr. Andrew Smellie
The Battle That Even Kings Lost: Dr. Raul Moreno
The Master Plan Of Evangelism: Robert Coleman
The Untold Story: Chronicles Of Modern-Day Christianity: Ron Harding
20/20 Book One: Dr. Timothy C. Kernan
20/20 Book Two: Dr. Timothy C. Kernan

Memory Scriptures

Class 1: Mark 1:35; Philippians 4:6
Class 2: Proverbs 11:30; 1 Peter 2:9-10
Class 3: Proverbs 3:5-6; 1 John 2:6
Class 4: Psalm 5:3; Acts 2:22-24
Class 5: Colossians 1:28-29; 1 Thessalonians 1:6-7
Class 6: Isaiah 32:8; Hebrews 3:13
Class 7: 1 Timothy 4:12; Ephesians 6:1-3
Class 8: Mark 6:7; Acts 14:1
Class 9: Philemon 1:6; Titus 2:7-8
Class 10: John 6:39; Acts 20:35
Class 11: 1 Timothy 6:18; Matthew 6:21
Class 12: Ezekiel 36:26; Proverbs 28:13

Preface
Selection Of Your Dodeka

1. **Select Trustworthy And Effective Leaders.** (Exodus 18:17-26)
    a. Choose Bible Talk Leaders who are effective.
    b. Choose Bible Talk Leaders who are trustworthy.
    c. Only have Bible Talk Leaders in your ministry that you believe can be trained to be fruitful and effective.
    d. A good selection of leaders satisfies the people.
    e. Not wear yourself out - better family life.
    f. Choosing the wrong leaders can have a devastating impact. Choosing the wrong people can cost you a generation. (Deuteronomy 1:20-28)

2. **Choosing Leaders Requires Prayer. Jesus Prayed All Night Before Selecting His Dodeka.** (Luke 6:12-16)
    a. Respect God and make prayerful and careful decisions. Act in haste, regret at leisure.
    b. God is not happy when He is not involved in the choices. (Hosea 8:4)

3. **Selection Of Leaders Is Spiritual.** (1 Samuel 16:1-13)
    a. God makes it clear to you when you must switch out leaders for lack of obedience to God.
    b. Make transitions prayerful, thoughtful, swift, and efficient. Constant transitions are a momentum killer. (Acts 1:24)
    c. God does not choose by outward appearance.

4. **Leaders Must Be Fruitful.** (Numbers 17:5-8)
   a. Fruitful disciples are prime candidates to be Bible Talk Leaders.
   b. If you put fruitful people in charge of a Bible Talk, it will be fruitful.
   c. Leaders must know their *First Principles Studies* before they can lead a Bible Talk. (Hebrews 5:11-14)
   d. Disciples must learn to be dedicated to an inspiring and daily lifestyle of setting up *First Principles Studies* with non-Christians.

5. **Leaders Must Be Able To Influence Their People.** (2 Corinthians 5:11)
   a. A leader must be able to have discussions that change people's hearts and thus their behavior. This is not as easy as it looks.
   b. If someone is not in studies, can this leader influence them to be in studies?
   c. If someone is not giving, can this leader influence them to give regularly?

6. **The Popular Choice Is Not Always The Best.** (Matthew 27:15-23)
   a. Do not be moved by the taunts of the crowd when choosing a leader.

7. **Choosing The Right Leaders - With The Right Priorities - Results In Rapid Expansion.** (Acts 6:1-7)
   a. The right people in the right place can cause a ministry to go from increasing to increasing rapidly.
   b. We must delegate tasks that others can do and focus on prayer and the ministry of the Word. (Acts 5:42, Acts 18:5)

8. **Leaders Must Be Reliable.** (2 Timothy 2:1-7)
   a. Without reliable workers, who are you going to work through? Your ministry will suffer and will not multiply.

9. **Bible Talk Leaders Must Not Be Hired Hands.** (John 10:1-15)
   a. Leadership is about love. Leaders should be people who love people.
   b. Your Bible Talk Leaders should become your best friends and the best friends of your members.
   c. Leaders must be trained to be healers and not conflict avoiders (Titus 1:10-16)

10. **Leaders Must Be Trained To Build Diverse Ministries.** (Matthew 28:19-20)
    a. Ministries should be attractive to a wide range of people. Cultural, racial, and personality differences should be used to benefit one another, not separate one another.

11. **Leaders Must Be Trained To Raise Missions Funds.** (2 Corinthians 9:1-5)
    a. The raising of funds is an essential skill in ministry. We learn this skill at the Bible Talk level.

12. **Choose Leaders Who Can Be Trained To Handle Persecution And Rejection.** (Revelation 2:13)
    a. Choose people who will not wilt under persecution.
    b. Cowardice is a sin that leaders to fruitlessness. (Revelation 21:8)

Study 1
Quiet Times

1. **Jesus Spent Time Alone With God.** (Mark 1:35)
   a. Have a quiet time every day.
   b. Give your first time of the day to God.

2. **We Talk To God In Our Quiet Times Through Prayer.** (Matthew 6:5-14)
   a. Prayer is essential. (Philippians 4:6)
   b. Prayer is powerful. (Mark 11:24)

3. **Humble Yourself And God Will Lift You Up.** (1 Peter 5:6)
   a. This is the only way for God to lift you up.
   b. Humbly and confidently focus on your shortcomings as a dearly loved child of God and God will lift you up.

4. **We Live On Every Word From The Mouth Of God.** (Matthew 4:1-11)
   a. God's Word gives us light, understanding, and direction. (Psalm 119:130-133)
   b. God's Word opens our eyes. (Ephesians 1:18-21)
   c. Bible study gives us faith. (Acts 17:10-12)
   d. Seek Godly wisdom from Christian books about the Bible. (Proverbs 4:5-9)
   e. God's Word will make you successful. (Joshua 1:8)

5. **When We Truly Connect To Jesus We Will Be Fruitful.** (John 15:1-8)
   a. Pray to the Lord of the Harvest to be fruitful. (Matthew 9:37-38)

6. **Fasting Is Rewarding.** (Matthew 6:16-17)
   a. Fasting can give focus and devotion to our worship.
   b. God responds to our fervent requests. God rewards our fast. (Isaiah 58:3, 9)

7. **God Looks At The Response To His Word.** (2 Kings 22)
   a. God is reading your heart when you are reading His Word.

8. **Singing Is Not Only For Sundays.** (Psalm 100:1-2)
   a. Singing at home, outdoors, and in nature is biblical worship.

9. **Get Out Into Nature And God's Creation.** (Romans 1:18-21)
   a. God's eternal power is clearly seen in His creation.

10. **Plan Your Schedule And Goals In Your Quiet Times.** (Proverbs 16:3)
    a. Your whole life is part of your worship.
    b. Plan your day, week, month, and year.
    c. Set your mind to accomplish goals.
    d. Plan to exercise, get work done, have excellent finances, etc., in your quiet time.

11. **Keep Wonder And Awe In Your Quiet Times.** (Hebrews 12:28-29)
    a. Get your confidence and joy from God. (Proverbs 14:26)

12. **Demolish All Negative And Faithless Thinking In Your Quiet Times.** (2 Corinthians 10:3-6)

a. List each and every negative thought you have and demolish it with a great Scripture. Be deliberate about this.
b. Completely trust God with your problems. (Proverbs 3:5-6)

Study 2
Personal Evangelism Skills

1. **Led By The Holy Spirit - Motivated By The Cross.** (2 Corinthians 5:11, 14-15)
   a. Evangelism is a way of life.
   b. The fear of the Lord also motivates us to save people from damnation.
   c. Jesus' love spiritually "forces" us to want to evangelize.

2. **Fruitfulness Is Maturity.** (Proverbs 11:30)
   a. Mature disciples are fruitful disciples.
   b. God wants us to have the fruits of the Spirit (Galatians 5:22-24), the fruit of our labor (Psalm 128:2), and the fruit of making disciples (2 Corinthians 5:20) so that we can be strong, healthy, and blessed.

3. **Schedule And Priorities Are Paramount.** (Acts 6:4)
   a. Make sure your schedule and priorities are all about fruitfulness.
   b. Have confirmed visitors for church and Bible Talks.
   c. Set up new conversion studies as often as possible to make sure that people are constantly coming to be baptized. (John 3:23)

4. **Know Your Rebuttals.** (1 Peter 3:15-16)
   a. When someone declines you, this is often an incredible opportunity to respectfully and gently refute the lies that keep them away from God.

b. Sharing your faith teaches you to refute atheism, materialism, etc.
   c. Share your heartfelt testimony. (1 Peter 2:9-10)
   d. We must not only tell people about church, but also declare God's praises who called us out of the darkness.

5. **There Is A Cost Of Fruitfulness.** (John 12:23-28)
   a. Hannah wept for it. (1 Samuel 1:10-19)
   b. Jesus wept for it. (Luke 22:44)
   c. Paul wept for it. (Romans 9:1-5)
   d. Crucify incompatible dreams and priorities.
   e. Share your faith every day. (Luke 19:47)

6. **The Promise of Fruitfulness.** (John 15:5)
   a. God is ready to make you fruitful. (Genesis 1:28)
   b. God is willing to make you fruitful. (1 Timothy 2:3-4)
   c. God can make you fruitful. (Acts 2:47; 1 Corinthians 3:6-7)

7. **Walk With Someone Who Is Effective.** (John 3:22)
   a. Fight to make your Bible Talk effective.
   b. Bring your studies to fruitful people.
   c. Make accountability conversational, not just a "report."

8. **Be Accountable In Your Evangelism.** (Mark 6:30)
   a. Accountability is from and expected by God. (Romans 14:12)
   b. Accountability - for the most part - is encouraging. (Luke 10:17)
   c. Accountability makes you sharp. (Proverbs 27:17)

9. **Be Relatable And Sincere In Your Evangelism.** (1 Corinthians 9:19-21)
    a. Be relatable.
    b. How is the ethnic and gender balance of your Bible Talk? (Revelation 7:9-10)
    c. Always get contact info to follow up.
    d. Make a friend - we baptize friends.
    e. Ask people about themselves.
    f. Relatableness leads to winning souls.

10. **You Can Only Reap What You Sow.** (Galatians 6:7-9)
    a. Persistence and perseverance are key.
    b. Take advantage of every opportunity. Do not give up.
    c. Do not fail to follow up. (John 5:14)
    d. Always be involved in multiple Bible Studies.

11. **Believe The Harvest Is Plentiful.** (Matthew 9:35-38)
    a. Do not try to judge who is open and who is not.
    b. Believe people are harassed and helpless.

12. **Stay Determined Under Persecution and Rejection.** (Luke 10:10-11, 16-17)
    a. Your heart will be attacked by rejection and persecution
    b. When was the last time you felt hurt by rejection or disappointment? Have you been open about it and sought help?
    c. Do not let your heart be wounded. This has taken out many would-be evangelizers.
    d. Pray for boldness. (Acts 4:29-31)
    e. What is hindering you from boldness? (Revelation 21:8)

Study 3
Conversion Study Skills

1. **Rely On God.** (Proverbs 3:5-6)
    a. Pray before you arrive at the study.
    b. Always start off the Bible study with a prayer.
    c. Ask for guidance, wisdom, and understanding from the Holy Spirit. God will give you insight.
    d. Have faith. Believe in your heart that the person will be baptized.

2. **Make A Disciple.** (1 John 2:6)
    a. Do not race through the studies. This is about thoroughly making a disciple who makes disciples for life. This is our goal and prayer for every person.
    b. Someone should be living as a disciple before they are baptized.
    c. After every study, you must call them to a decision. (Deuteronomy 32:46-47) Are they willing to seek God with all their heart? Are they willing to make the Bible their standard? Do they want to be a disciple, etc.?

3. **Believe You Are God's Ambassador.** (Isaiah 6: 1-8)
    a. God calls you to be a leader. If Jesus was a leader, should you be a leader?
    b. God gives us a powerful ability to see people and the stumbling blocks and challenges for the non-Christian to make it. (2 Corinthians 2:11)

      c. Faith is an essential ingredient in any conversion. You must believe God is with you and will use you and others to impact studies. (Acts 26:17-18)
      d. Preach with an expectation of obedience.

4. **Excel At Bible Studies.** (2 Timothy 2:15)
      a. Be sure to have a follow-up talk with the disciples who were in the study to discuss what could have been done better.
      b. Read Scriptures and books about relationships and connecting effectively with people.

5. **Be Sure Everyone Has A Role.** (Ephesians 4:16)
      a. Do you know who in your ministry can lead studies all the way through? Are they designated and stacked with studies?
      b. Not everyone should be a dynamic leader. We also need empathetic and sincere friends and the dutiful note-taker to forge a team.
      c. If it would help, include people from other economic, cultural, and ethnic backgrounds in the studies. (James 2:1)
      d. Create a "family" or team that will "gang tackle" this person and "rescue" them into the Kingdom of God.
      e. Great engaging and stimulating questions are essential to invite wholesome discussion that includes everyone.
      f. Everyone should follow the Bible Study Leader in their communication and engagement.

6. **Choose Your Environment.** (1 Peter 4:9)

a. Choose a quiet place with good lighting where someone can be open without worrying about who is listening.
   b. Sometimes, a beverage, snack, and even a candle can make a huge difference in someone's comfort level.
   c. Many people are going to relate to your body language as much as what you say. (It is unacceptable to be unenthusiastic, late, to dress inappropriately, and/or to have lousy hygiene.)

7. **Read The Scriptures Appropriately With Reverence And Heart.** (1 Peter 4:11)
   a. God's Word is exciting, and the life of a disciple is too. It is a sin to read the Bible in an unexciting, boring way. Use inflection, emphasize keywords, pronounce words correctly, recognize biblical punctuation. (Hebrews 12:28)
   b. Know the study you are leading very well.
   c. Stay on track and gently redirect back to the Scriptures when veering off happens.
   d. Keep illustrations short and appropriate to that person.
   e. Strive to keep each study under an hour. Be considerate of time. The exception is *The Light And Darkness Study,* which may be up to two hours.

8. **Connect And Listen.** (James 1:19)
   a. Give the person you are studying with a Bible and inscribe it as a gift.
   b. Connect before you correct. (Proverbs 20:5; 1 Thessalonians 2:8) Get to know about the life

of the person with whom you are studying. Who they are? Where they come from? Religious background, etc.? Make a timeline of their religious lives. (Example questions to build a timeline are at the end of this study.)
   c. After reading a Scripture, ask your study what they understand from it before you teach and call to decision. Then go back and listen to what they understand from your teaching when you are done.
   d. Do not assume. They may not know or understand everything you explained; ask questions, draw out their hearts, and then give direction and challenges. (Proverbs 18:13)
   e. Everyone should empathize and listen, even if they are not leading the study.
   f. Hang out and communicate between studies.
   g. Be vulnerable, not combative or arrogant.
   h. Be wise and do not bring in new people when reading the sin list or being very vulnerable.
   i. Choose the discipler for your convert from those who connect the best.
   j. Ask questions to help you make appropriate analogies.
   k. The more they talk, the better.
   l. You are in a tug of war between this person and the world. It is all about relationships.

9. **Keep The *First Principles Studies* Clear And Focused.** (2 Timothy 1:13)
   a. Set up "custom studies" between the conversion studies if necessary but do not veer from each study's point.
   b. Do not challenge on things you have not taught yet. One step at a time.

10. **Do Not Let The Study Or Your Evangelism Flounder.** (1 Corinthians 15:58)
    a. Many disciples can be in multiple studies every week. What do you have to change to be in more studies? Priorities? Schedule?
    b. At the end of every study, set up the following study with a date, time, and location.
    c. Bring in your leader to deal with difficult situations and keep things moving.
    d. Do not stop sharing your faith because you have someone studying. The harvest is plentiful. Keep an eye on having fruit in the future.

11. **Be Happy Under Persecution and Rejection.** (Matthew 5:11-12)
    a. You will be insulted, persecuted, and slandered as a true disciple of Jesus.
    b. Always be open about your hurts, pray and seek true healing from God so you can continue to seek and save the lost.

12. **Timeline Example:**
    1. **When did you become a Christian?**
    2. **When did you become a disciple? (Who made you into one?)**
    3. **When did you have a saving relationship with God and how?**
    4. **When did you receive the "forgiveness of sins?" (How?)**
    5. **When did you receive the "Holy Spirit?" (How?)**
    6. **When were you in darkness? (Why?)**
    7. **When did you enter the light? (How?)**

8. When did you repent of all your sins?
9. When did you become a part of the Kingdom?
10. When were you baptized? Why were you baptized?
11. When were you born again? (How? Why?)
12. When did you die with Christ? (How?)
13. When did you get added to the body?
14. When did you confess *"Jesus as Lord?"*
15. When did you pray Jesus into your heart? (Trick question)

Study 4
Counting The Cost Skills

Note: Subpoints (a, b, c, etc.) are formatted as questions to ask the person with whom you are studying.

1. **Why Count The Cost?** (Luke 14:25-33)
    a. Why does God want us to count the cost of following Him and think through what it will take to be a committed disciple for life?
    b. What has changed in your heart and life during the time we have been studying the Bible?
    c. What has been your greatest challenge so far?
    d. Are there any areas of life that you are holding back from surrendering to Jesus? (Matthew 22:35-40)
    e. Do you see discipleship as a lifetime commitment? (Luke 9:62)
    f. Why do you want to be a disciple?

2. **Jesus Is Lord And Savior.** (Acts 2:22-24)
    a. Who is Jesus? God in the flesh. (John 1:1-14)
    b. What does "Lordship" mean? (Galatians 2:20)
    c. Jesus died for your sins and was resurrected on the third day. (1 Corinthians 15:3-5)
    d. Why do we say, *"Jesus is Lord?"* (Romans 10:9-13; Acts 22:16)

3. **Baptism Is For The Forgiveness Of Sins.** (Acts 2:36-38)
    a. Baptism is necessary for salvation. (Mark 16:16, Colossians 2:11-12)

- b. Baptism for the forgiveness of sins is by submersion in water. (Acts 8:38)
- c. One must repent - be made into a disciple - before baptism. (Matthew 28:18-20)
- d. If someone believed in Jesus, repented, but was not baptized, could they be saved? Why? (Romans 3:23-25; Acts 2:38; Romans 6:1-6)

4. **Quiet Times.** (Psalm 5:1-3)
    - a. There is nothing more important in your schedule than your daily time with God. (2 Peter 1:5-9)
    - b. Read the Bible daily (Acts 17:11-12); Pray daily (Luke 11:1-4). Occasionally, take time to sing, journal, and read spiritual books such as the ones on the Suggested Resource List.

5. **Discipling.** (Hebrews 3:13)
    - a. What does "Discipleship" mean? (Mark 1:14-18; Matthew 28:18-20)
    - b. Seeking advice. (Proverbs 19:20)
    - c. Daily contact. (Hebrews 3:12-13)
    - d. Follow Up Studies - Let's set one up right now.
    - e. Your discipler (discipleship partner) is _____. (This person should be in the studies.) Have the future disciple commit to a set weekly time with his/her discipler.
    - f. The church is a family. (Acts 2:42-47)
    - g. New Members Orientation. The next one is _____.
    - h. Your Bible Talk is _____.

6. **Conflict Resolution.** (Matthew 18:15-17)

a. A mature approach to dealing with sin and conflict is to have a critical eye but not a critical heart. (2 Timothy 2:22-26)
   b. Settle matters quickly so that sin is rooted out and any resentment or bitterness is avoided.
   c. Do not have a worldly victim mentality. Take responsibility to help resolve any conflicts. (Matthew 5:25)
   d. Speak the truth in love. (Ephesians 4:15) Hate the sin: love the sinner. (1 Peter 4:8)
   e. You will have conflict and hurts in the church, but it is no reason to leave.

7. **Repentance And Confession Of Sins.** (1 John 1:5-10)
   a. Do not let Satan get a foothold. (James 5:16)
   b. We have genuine friendships with each other when we walk in the light.
   c. What does "Repentance" mean? (Luke 13:1-5, Acts 26:20)

8. **Meetings Of The Body.** (Hebrews 10:23-25)
   a. Your Bible Talk, Your Region/House Church, Your Ministry (Singles, Marrieds, Campus, Teens), Midweek Services are the *"meetings of the body"* - the Kingdom. (Matthew 6:33)
   b. Look through the church calendar and website.

9. **Evangelism.** (Matthew 28:18-20)
   a. Daily lifestyle of evangelism. (Acts 5:42)
   b. Show no partiality in your evangelism. We want a diverse ministry that imitates the demographics of the city in which the church is located. (James 2:1)

10. **Giving.** (Malachi 3:6-12)

a. Why should we give? Do you have the ability to give generously? (1 Timothy 6:17; 2 Corinthians 9:6-11)
  b. Do your "life skills" need work? (Deuteronomy 8:18)
  c. What is "Benevolence?" This is given at Midweek Services. (James 2:16-17)
  d. What is "Special Missions?" (2 Corinthians 9:1-5)
  e. What is your pledge that you want to generously give each week?
  f. Do you know how to donate online? (1 Timothy 6:17)

11. **Dating.** (2 Corinthians 6:14-18)
    a. Disciples date and marry disciples because biblically believer = disciple.
    b. "Encouragement Dates" are mutual edification and getting to know your brothers and sisters. This protects one another. (1 Timothy 5:1-2)
    c. Dating and marriage are hopes, but heaven is the goal.

12. **Persecution.** (2 Timothy 3:12)
    a. Persecution is guaranteed for every disciple and comes in many forms.
    b. From where will your greatest persecution come?
    c. What do you do when you are persecuted? (Acts 5:41-42)

Last Question: What is the most difficult aspect of your life to give up, or what will be the most difficult challenge for you as a disciple? Honor God! Do not baptize anyone if you can talk them out of it!

Study 5
Discipling Skills

1. **Jesus Is The Standard.** (Colossians 1:28-29)
    a. Use the Bible in discipling. (2 Timothy 3:16-17)
    b. Discipling is about disciples being more like Jesus. We need to be taught to be more like Jesus.
    c. God gives us the energy we need to disciple people.
    d. Discipling is for everyone.
    e. Discipling is not about being a better you; it is about being like Jesus.
    f. Discipling is guiding the heart to have Jesus' lifestyle and priorities.

2. **Discipling Is About Teaching How To Be A Follower Of Christ And Fisherman.** (Mark 1:16-17)
    a. The calling to be a disciple has always been the call to be a fisher of men.
    b. Have accountability for evangelism, visitors, and studies.
    c. Make accountability conversational, not just a "report."
    d. Go sharing together and be in studies together.
    e. Evangelism allows God to give you everything you need - people, funds to hire leaders, houses for meetings, and even vehicles for transportation… Everything to make more disciples.

3. **Discipling Meets The Needs Of The Church.** (Exodus 18:13-27)

a. Each person in your ministry can have all of their needs met if everyone is in discipling relationships.
   b. Discipling is God's plan to meet the needs of the whole world.

4. **Discipling Is A Responsibility.** (Hebrews 3:12-13)
   a. We are responsible for taking care of one another.
   b. Is everyone in our ministry being discipled?
   c. Do you have a "discipleship partner tree?"

5. **Discipling Is Family.** (1 Thessalonians 2:7-8, 11)
   a. Discipling is part of how we show care for one another.
   b. As one family, there should be no "clergy/laity divide."

6. **Discipling Is Imitation.** (1 Thessalonians 1:4-8)
   a. Seek advice before making decisions.
   b. Do not reinvent the wheel. (Hebrews 13:7)
   c. Disciples must be reliable. (2 Timothy 2:2)
   d. Our example gives us the authority to call others to obedience.
   e. Our humility expressed in openness about our sins and shortcomings will inspire those we disciple to be equally open.

7. **In Discipling, People Must Be Drawn Out.** (Proverbs 20:5)
   a. It is important to ask many questions in discipling.
   b. Build friendships.
   c. Have empathy and compassion.
   d. You must believe in your disciples.

8. **Give People Authority In Your Life.** (Hebrews 13:17)
   a. The example of Elijah and Elisha. (1 Kings 19:19-21)
   b. Obedience to authority is biblical.
   c. Giving someone authority over your life can be frightening, but God is still in control.

9. **We Will Always Need Discipling.** (Matthew 28:18-20)
   a. Discipling teaches us to obey everything Jesus commanded us.
   b. We do not mature beyond our need for discipling. We always face fresh challenges and need fresh discipling, though older Christians need to ***"train themselves to distinguish good from evil."*** (Hebrews 5:14)
   c. Women need female discipling even when they become married, and their husband becomes their main discipler. (Titus 2:3-5)

10. **Disciple Character Into People.** (Hebrews 12:4-7)
    a. So many people lacked parenting and were never taught character and life skills. Do not assume people know about these things.
    b. You must teach them integrity, honor, self-respect, etc. Consider making character studies for your disciples that meet their needs.

11. **Our Attitude Towards Discipling Should Be:**
    a. Proverbs 9:8, Proverbs 10:17, Proverbs 12:1, Proverbs 12:15, Proverbs 13:1, Proverbs 13:10, Proverbs 15:5, Proverbs 15:10, Proverbs 15:12, Proverbs 15:31, Proverbs 15:32, Proverbs 17:10, Proverbs 19:20, Proverbs 20:18, Proverbs 25:12,

Proverbs 27:5, Proverbs 27:9, Proverbs 28:23, Proverbs 29:1.

12. **Discipling Is About Love.** (1 Peter 4:8)
    a. Above all, discipling should be loving and gentle. (Galatians 6:1)
    b. Remember to fear the Lord as a discipler. Do not be harsh or use ungodly methods of motivation, or God will be harsh with you. (Psalm 18:26)

Study 6
Bible Talk Leadership Skills

1. **Bible Talk Is Family.** (1 Thessalonians 2:7-12)
    a. Remember, Bible Talk is not just a meeting, it is a family with a weekly meeting. Family is of God, and family is what God desires for every one of His children.
    b. Build diversity into your Bible Talk. (1 Corinthians 12:15-19)
    c. Bible Talk is the "living room of the church." Do not be shy to have fun family times.
    d. Have a great name for your Bible Talk.
    e. Every Bible Talk should have a geographic charge.
    f. Have a clear membership.
    g. Visit your members' homes and know their life stories.
    h. Believe in each person in your Bible Talk and have a role for them, including a right-hand person or couple. (Ephesians 4:11-12)
    i. Ask for loyalty and give loyalty.

2. **Have The Conviction: Every Bible Talk Fruitful.** (John 15:1-8)
    a. A conviction is not just a feeling but a deeply held belief that does not waiver. (1 Thessalonians 1:4)
    b. Ensure that everyone knows or learns the *First Principles Studies* thoroughly. (Hebrews 5:11-14)
    c. As a Bible Talk Leader have a schedule and priorities that allow you to be in many studies. (Acts 6:4)

d. God's Word always comes back fruitful. (Isaiah 55:10-11)
   e. You can go to campus or the mall and have as many evangelistic "Bible Talk" meetings as you want. Gather, have a motivating huddle up, pray, go sharing, then come back for a Bible discussion and turn visitors into Bible studies. Do this as often as you wish.

3. **Bible Talk Leaders Pray, Call The Play, And Lead The Way.** (Isaiah 32:8)
   a. Set faithful and challenging goals for spiritual health, fruitfulness, growth, and raising money for missions.
   b. Remember your goals and accomplish your goals with God.
   c. Bible Talk Leaders are goal setters and "play makers." (Isaiah 32:8)
   d. Bible Talk Leaders take full responsibility and ownership of the effectiveness of their Bible Talk.
   e. Bible Talk Leaders need to be humble and to get help when they need it.

4. **Bible Talk Life Is Daily.** (Hebrews 3:13)
   a. Remember the ministry is about a daily walk with God: Daily quiet times, evangelism, contact with disciples, serving the needy, etc.
   b. Call everyone to an "everyday - house to house" schedule and lifestyle on campus (Acts 19:9b) and in the neighborhood. (Acts 20:20)
   c. Have you introduced yourself to all your neighbors and/or classmates? (Colossians 4:5, Acts 5:42)

5. **Lead By Example And Humility.** (1 Peter 5:2-3)
    a. Be an example of everything you want others to do. Have visitors to Bible Talk, be punctual, etc.
    b. You may be the only Bible people read.
    c. Admit your shortcomings and share humbly about your progress. (1 Timothy 4:15)

6. **Be Accountable.** (Mark 6:30)
    a. Share how your Bible Talk went with your discipler: good, bad, and ugly. Do not make anyone chase you for the information.
    b. Be willing to change time, location, theme, etc., to get more fruit.
    c. Bible Talk Leaders are accountable for the members of their Bible Talk, the number of visitors, and the number of studies they currently have.
    d. As a minister, believe that the accountability of each of your Bible Talks is a necessity and will help them to achieve their goals.
    e. What you focus on is what you get.

7. **Keep Everyone Up To Date.** (Philippians 2:2)
    a. At the end of Bible Talk, the leader should share about the next opportunity to come to church, a retreat, etc.
    b. Use chats, text, and other means of communication to keep your Bible Talk and/or your ministry in the know.

8. **Remember The Power of Hospitality.** (Hebrews 13:2)
    a. Make your meetings smell, taste, sound, feel, and look great.

b. Show up ready to serve. (Philippians 2:6-7)
   c. The meeting of the Bible Talk is primarily for guests to be taught the Word of God.
   d. Do not use "Kingdom lingo" in your meetings with visitors present.

9. **Plan To Split Your Bible Talk.** (2 Timothy 2:2)
   a. To multiply your Bible Talk, have as many baptisms as members, raise up the next leader, and split it in half.
   b. Bible Talks can be clustered together into "House Churches." Each House Church should have responsible leaders who can lead their Bible Talk and help oversee others.
   c. The local church leaders must build this empowering structure.

10. **Discipling Happens Within The Bible Talk.** (Hebrews 10:24-25)
    a. Alternate from time to time d-groups (discipling groups) and d-times (discipling times) so everyone is involved and connected. (Colossians 3:16)
    b. Everyone in the Bible Talk should have their primary discipler in the Bible Talk. (1 Corinthians 14:40)
    c. No cross discipling between Bible Talks; it disempowers the Bible Talk Leaders.
    d. Care about disciples' marriages and/or dating lives and overall well-being. (James 2:16)

11. **Disciple Sin And Conflict Quickly And Completely.** (Hebrews 12:14-15; Matthew 5:25)
    a. Strengthen your most vulnerable person, and you strengthen your whole Bible Talk.

- b. When someone does not show up to Bible Talk or call to let the Bible Talk Leader know they cannot come, this is concerning and must be addressed. The Bible Talk Leader is responsible for making sure his/her whole Bible Talk is at all meetings of the body. (Hebrews 10:24-25)
- c. Confessing sin brings victory. (Joshua 7:16-26)
- d. Bring in Shepherds to help if you are having difficulty or long-standing issues. (James 5:20)

12. **Stay Gritty Under Persecution And Rejection.** (John 15:18-21)
    - a. Prepare your Bible Talk to receive persecution and attacks.
    - b. Teach at Bible Talk, on occasion, about how Jesus and the church were persecuted.

Study 7
The Teen Ministry

1. **Teen Leaders Must Be Heroes.** (1 Timothy 4:12)
    a. In the eyes of the teens, if you are not a hero you are a zero.
    b. The teen ministry is a chance to raise up future campus leaders.
    c. Teen Leaders should be able to relate to the teens and be a great example.
    d. Teen Leaders should have a car in a city where that is necessary.
    e. Teen Leaders need to feel honored to be in the teen ministry.

2. **Devos And Bible Talks Need To Be Awesome.** (Mark 6:42)
    a. Great food, pure music, and fun. Teens eat a lot, so food is a gateway to their hearts.
    b. Make sure to have a great location. (Acts 14:1)
    c. Go to where the teens are: malls, parks, arcades, and/or coffee shops for d-times and sharing times. (Acts 16:13)
    d. Have fun sports and games at outings.

3. **Relatable Topics And Trends.** (Acts 17:21)
    a. At d-time, devo, or even in the car, make sure conversation is relatable and engaging.
    b. Paul was able to talk to people on "their level." (1 Corinthians 9:19-22)
    c. Lessons should use current events and be easily relatable.
    d. Know the lingo, songs, and gestures of teens.

  e. You will know your lesson was impactful if they continue to talk about it for the remainder of the week.

4. **Persistence And Perseverance.** (Acts 18:9-10)
    a. Stay the course every day, and you will eventually have a breakthrough.
    b. Teens can be up and down. You must be solid. (Galatians 6:2)

5. **Expect Teens To Be Disciples And Workers.** (Mark 1:16-18)
    a. A baptized teen disciple is not a "boy" or "girl" but a young man or a young woman.
    b. Call the teens to be evangelistic.
    c. A teen that is not evangelistic is a teen that will eventually fall away.
    d. Raise up teenage leaders to lead other teens.
    e. A goal for the teen ministry is to have a few teen-led Bible Talks.

6. **Fight For The Relationship.** (1 Corinthians 9:22)
    a. Get into their heart and their homes.
    b. Win their trust and be a friend.
    c. Spend time consistently.
    d. No one cares how much you know until they know how much you care.

7. **Social Media Outreach.** (Colossians 4:5)
    a. Use and be familiar with Facebook, Instagram, Twitter, TikTok, etc.
    b. Get help from teens in this area.
    c. Satan knows how to use these social media platforms.

8. **Get Teens Involved In Their High School.** (Acts 17:19)
    a. Have each teen disciple get involved in at least one extracurricular activity.
    b. This makes them more influential, and they will have more friends to invite to church.
    c. Consider starting a Christian club. This may allow for resources and money for your outreach.

9. **Relationship With Teens' Parents.** (Ephesians 6:1-3)
    a. Create and give out to parents updated calendars, as well as to the teens.
    b. Communicate and get permission for teens to attend meetings.
    c. Connect parents with the Shepherding Couples.

10. **Expect And Implement Discipleship.** (John 8:31-32)
    a. Have consistent and meaningful d-times and quiet times.
    b. Teach life skills, including how to save to contribute to the weekly contribution and missions.
    c. Fight hard to baptize Kingdom kids. (2 Timothy 1:5)
    d. Encourage older disciples to bring any teens they know.
    e. Teach the teens to be respectful of older people.

11. **Set Correct Expectations.** (Matthew 28:20)
    a. For teens make midweek optionally as their midweek is the Friday or Saturday devotional.

    b. Teens need to get great grades to glorify God and to please their parents. (Colossians 3:23-24)
    c. Do not exasperate the teens by expecting perfection. (Ephesians 6:4)

12. **Peer Pressure and Persecution.** (1 Peter 4:3-4)
    a. Always teach the teens how to deal with bullying, persecution, and rejection.
    b. Train them to resist godless choices and temptations at school.

Study 8
The Campus Ministry

1. **The Campus Campaign.** (1 Samuel 18:16)
    a. Start with a bang. Pray hard. All night prayer? Jericho march prayer around campus? Early morning prayer meetings? Prayer chains?
    b. Blitz! Share with tons of people at the beginning and get tons of studies going.
    c. Follow-up is crucial: Have a "follow up party" leading into a "Campus Bring Your Neighbor Day."
    d. Share and study with opinion leaders - student body officers, club presidents, athletes, fraternity and sorority members, etc. (Acts 18:24-28)
    e. Campus ministry couples should purchase their university hats and merchandise.

2. **Numerical Faith And Effort Goals.** (Luke 13:32)
    a. "Prayer goals save souls." Motivate and inspire your ministry to be excited about prayer goals.
    b. From time to time, have daily sharing goals, visitors, and studies goals. Make it fun and exciting.
    c. Have challenging but realistic prayer goals. Through the power of God, hit your goals.
    d. Set baptism and expansion prayer goals. How many new Bible Talk Leaders will be raised up and how many new Bible Talks will be started?
    e. Additions are baptisms and restorations. Multiplication is new Bible Talks.

3. **Campus Run Services.** (1 Timothy 4:12-13)
   a. Have the students prepare and run a Sunday service calling it "Campus Sunday."
   b. Train each speaker on how to present publicly and how to preach or share. This will increase their confidence and competence. (1 Timothy 4:13)
   c. Encourage the people to show up in their university gear for the campus service.

4. **Adapt.** (1 Corinthians 9:22)
   a. Be willing to change your time and location to maximize visitors.
   b. Go where the fish are: Have multiple Bible Talks on campus throughout the week.
   c. Use social media to make new contacts and to share your faith.

5. **Solomon's Colonnade.** (Acts 5:12)
   a. Establish a disciple hangout.
   b. The campus ministry couple should put in the hours at "Solomon's Colonnade" in fellowship and in doing studies.
   c. Strive to have the campus students live in the dorms so Bible Talks can be held in the dorms.

6. **Print And Social Media.** (Colossians 4:4-6)
   a. Have great personal invites and ministry flyers.
   b. Think about having a name and a logo for the campus ministry, as well as shirts, wristbands, and other merchandise that will help propagate your ministry name.
   c. Teach the importance and impact of social media. Fry the airwaves.

7. **Campus Disciples' Personal Example.** (1 Corinthians 11:1)
    a. Grades - Sit in the front of the classroom and involve yourself. This may bring people to you seeking academic help as well as life help.
    b. Lifestyle - Be outgoing! Read books on a variety of topics and get involved in extracurricular campus life to meet more people. Do not be a "moody millennial."
    c. Fitness - Gain the respect of even the most disciplined athletes on campus and watch the fruit come in.
    d. Seek racial and gender balance in your ministry. (Colossians 3:11)
    e. Spiritual example - Expect campus disciples to be an example of purity and to call out the sin on campus.
    f. Sincerity in friendship. Care about those you are studying with even if they do not make it. Have friendship times outside of studies.

8. **Group Evangelism.** (Mark 6:7)
    a. Jesus sent His disciples out two by two.
    b. Keep each other accountable when one is tempted to "chicken out."
    c. Allows us to be bolder.
    d. Group evangelism can make evangelism fun.

9. **Food, Fun, And Fellowship.** (Acts 2:46)
    a. Food always attracts students.
    b. Plan powerful Friday night devotionals and fellowship with great food and appropriate music after devo.
    c. Happy disciples are fruitful disciples.

d. Plan retreats and outings i.e., camping, beach days, sporting events, etc.

10. **Relevant And Engaging Bible Talks.** (Acts 14:1)
    a. Discuss hot topics. Be familiar with current events.
    b. Use humor.
    c. Keep the Bible Talk to less than an hour.
    d. Set up studies right after the discussion is over.
    e. In some Bible Talks directly refute false doctrines.

11. **Clubs.** (Acts 8:4-13)
    a. Consider founding a Christian Club, as they can give you access to funds, resources, and facilities.

12. **Stay Gritty.** (Luke 6:27-36)
    a. Persecution can be heavy on campus.
    b. Prepare your people with the right attitude. (Luke 6:22-23)

At devo, roleplay a model campus Bible Talk and give feedback.

Study 9
The Marrieds / Singles Ministry

1. **The Marrieds And Singles Bible Talks Are All About Having An Evangelistic Lifestyle.** (Philemon 1:6)
    a. Evangelism is daily. Live the schedule and priorities of evangelism. (Acts 5:42)
    b. Ideally, every disciple has a personal visitor to each Bible Talk.

2. **Evangelism And Hospitality Sounds Great.** (Luke 4:32)
    a. Have well-prepared lessons.
    b. Meet in a quiet place where people can share openly and listen carefully without distractions.

3. **Evangelism And Hospitality Feels Great.** (Romans 16:16)
    a. Warm welcomes.
    b. Welcoming atmosphere.

4. **Evangelism And Hospitality Tastes Great.** (Genesis 18:6-8)
    a. Amazing food.
    b. Abundant drinks.

5. **Evangelism And Hospitality Smells Great.** (Psalm 51:7)
    a. Be physically and spiritually clean.

    b. Clean households and snacks smell great.

6. **Evangelism And Hospitality Looks Great.** (Luke 22:12)
   a. Seasonal decorations and family pictures are welcoming and reassuring.
   b. Good lighting is essential.

7. **Evangelism And Hospitality Have A Great Time and Location.** (Ecclesiastes 3:1)
   a. Choose your time and location carefully to maximize visitors. (Acts 3:1)
   b. Friday nights are often great for marrieds and singles as people do not have to run off to get ready for work the next day.

8. **Be A Personal Example.** (Titus 2:7-8)
   a. Be a respectable member of your community and workplace.
   b. Be impressive to the visitors by your humility.

9. **Babysitting And Family Coordination.** (1 Timothy 3:4-5)
   a. Plan in advance how your family and children will be taken care of during Bible Talk.
   b. Help visitors to get the child care they need in order to come to the Bible Talk.

10. **Will Your Bible Talk Be "Mingles" Or Marrieds Or Singles Or Gender Based?** (1 Corinthians 7:34)
    a. Is your Bible Talk going to be mixed? All women? All men? All Marrieds? All Singles?
    b. What will catch more fish?

11. **Tie Your Members Into Their Ministry.** (Titus 2:1-8)
    a. Regardless of your ministry breakdown, make sure your Singles, Marrieds, men, and women are connected to their respective ministries so they can get their needs met.

12. **Stand Firm.** (Acts 4:18-22)
    a. Prepare your Bible Talk for persecution and trouble

At devo or the Winter Workshop, roleplay a model Bible Talk and give feedback.

Study 10
Shepherding Skills

1. **Good Shepherd Vs. Hired Hand.** (John 10:11-13)
   a. The sheep must know you well, and you must know them.
   b. Protect the sheep with your life.
   c. Connect personally with everyone.

2. **Leaders Are Shepherds And Must Be Examples: Good Disciples And Healthy People.** (1 Peter 5:1-4)
   a. Daily Quiet Times.
   b. Great relationships with their disciplers.
   c. Physical health.
   d. Hard workers at their jobs.
   e. Growing in all of the fruits of the Spirit.
   f. Building a loving physical family.
   g. Leading a fruitful and dynamic Bible Talk.
   h. Growing in their knowledge of the Word.
   i. Leading by example; being humble and being open about areas of shortcomings.

3. **Shepherds Promote Spirituality.** (Galatians 6:7-10)
   a. The dog you feed is the dog that will grow.
   b. Strengthen disciples from the inside.
   c. Bad habits and vices will lead to fallaways.
   d. Jesus taught self-denial to prevent us from feeding the wrong dog.

4. **Shepherds Strengthen Disciples By Getting Them Into The Fight For Souls.** (2 Chronicles 16:9)

- a. Just because you are devoted to "prayer and the ministry of the Word" does not mean your people necessarily are.
- b. God strengthens disciples when they are in the battle.
- c. Disciples can often be strengthened more by getting into the battle for souls than by rest.

5. **Appointed Shepherds Take Responsibility For Retention.** (John 6:39)
    - a. Evangelists and Women's Ministry Leaders should be primarily concerned about baptisms and restorations. Shepherding Couples should be primarily concerned about the retention of the membership.
    - b. The Shepherding Couples must find ways to help and encourage the most vulnerable members.
    - c. Growth is both adding and retaining. (Titus 1:5)

6. **Practice And Teach Hospitality.** (Hebrews 13:2)
    - a. Hospitality is encouragement and can be very strengthening. (1 Peter 4:8)
    - b. Every Bible Talk must be made into a family through hospitality.

7. **Shepherds Bring Order.** (Titus 1:9-11)
    - a. When dealing with issues, get the facts and both sides of the story. (Proverbs 18:17)
    - b. Know your doctrine and be able to refute false doctrine.
    - c. Sin disrupts households.

8. **Heal And Resolve - Do Not React.** (2 Timothy 2:22-26)
   a. Be kind to everyone, able to teach, not resentful.
   b. Gently instruct those who oppose you.
   c. Do not quarrel but be kind.
   d. Treat others as you want to be treated. (Matthew 7:12)
   e. Treat older people with respect and love. (1 Peter 5:5)
   f. Get excited about being a peacemaker. (Matthew 5:9)

9. **Respect And Protect The Weak.** (Acts 20:35)
   a. Build up those who are weak.
   b. Know the difference between those who are weak and those who are lukewarm. (Revelation 3:14-20)

10. **Beware Of The Bitter Root That Defiles.** (Hebrews 12:14-16)
    a. Bitterness is hurt left unforgiven.
    b. Defilement is the loss of the heart of a child. (Matthew 18:3)
    c. Satan's weapon of mass destruction is bitterness: Many can be defiled.
    d. Hurt can lead to a "man focus" thus taking your eyes off of God. Make people small and God big. (Psalm 37:7-9)
    e. Learn to pour burning coals. (Romans 12:9-21)
    f. Be able to get hit with "friendly fire" and live. We are on the same team fighting against Satan. Choose not to be easily offended. (Proverbs 12:16)

11. **Deal With Sin In A Godly Way.** (Matthew 18:15-17)
    a. Talk personally with everyone involved, not through other parties.
    b. Restore the weak gently; teach and help them carry their load. (Galatians 6:1-5)

12. **Stay Gritty And Encourage Disciples Who Are Persecuted.** (2 Timothy 4:1-5)
    a. Preach the Word even "out of season" during persecution.
    b. Keep your head in all circumstances.

Study 11
Fund Raising Skills

1. **Command Generosity.** (1 Timothy 6:18)
   a. Teach people that God wants them to be generous.
   b. Do not store up for yourselves. (Matthew 6:19)
   c. Train people to live under their means.
   d. Suggest MERCY*worldwide* Life Skills training for those in debt.

2. **Teach The Why Of Weekly And Missions Giving.** (2 Corinthians 9: 1-7)
   a. There is no need to write about this because every disciple should be willing to give.
   b. In the first century, the church leadership had the authority to call for funds to be raised for special purposes. In this case, a famine in Jerusalem; in our case, evangelizing the world and training leaders.

3. **See Fundraising As A Way To Strengthen Your Ministry.** (Matthew 6:21)
   a. Your ministry's heart will be where its money is.
   b. Faithfully and responsibly hitting your goal unifies the ministry and helps people put their heart in the Kingdom.
   c. God gives us the ability to give. (1 Chronicles 29:14)
   d. God's generosity should move us. (Luke 5:1-11)

e. Fundraising does not make anyone struggle. It shows they are struggling.

4. **Pray And Fast For God's Will And Plans For Your Ministry.** (Proverbs 16:3)
   a. What mission teams are going out? Who needs to be trained?
   b. When you know what God wants you to do, then you know your goals.
   c. When you communicate in detail God's plans, people will sacrifice and be generous to achieve them.
   d. Proclaim the plan and the dream.

5. **Cover God's Inspiring Plan And Dream With A Financial Goal.** (Luke 5:1-11)
   a. Make sure everyone understands the inspiring and important needs.
   b. Be sure everyone understands the financial goal that will cover those needs.

6. **Cover God's Financial Goal With Faithful Pledges.** (Luke 16:10)
   a. Individually go from disciple to disciple for them to give you their weekly and/or missions pledge.
   b. Make sure that your pledges in your ministry are more than your needs and your goal.
   c. Lead the way.
   d. Make sure every Bible Talk is responsible for their total goal.
   e. By failing to plan, you are planning to fail.

7. **Cover Your Pledges With Creative Fundraising Ideas.** (Exodus 12:36)

    a. Find creative ways to raise funds.
    b. Make sure everyone has a pledge, and also a plan to hit their pledges.
    c. When some give a lot more than others, this can reveal division in the ministry that needs to be healed.
    d. Rushing missions collection at the last minute can be very discouraging.

8. **Be Disciplined In Your Giving And Final Completion Date.** (Ecclesiastes 5:4)
    a. Keep to your plan and be disciplined in turning in your missions giving.
    b. Make sure everyone gives what they can right away and does not wait for the end.
    c. Counting the cost is different than paying the price.

9. **Teach On Accountability.** (Hebrews 10:24-25)
    a. Preach about accountability every few months.
    b. Honor by publically lifting up those who show faithfulness in their giving, as well as those that raise remarkable amounts. (Psalm 15:4)
    c. If anyone flounders, give them a plan.
    d. Jesus watches the giving. (Mark 12:41-42)

10. **Share Progress And Good News.** (Psalms 96:3)
    a. Share how your ministry is doing in your fundraising efforts.
    b. Celebrate the victory.
    c. Thank people for their giving.

11. **Hit Your Goal Early And Help Other Bible Talks Hit Their Goal.** (Luke 6:38)
    a. Plan to give more than is needed.

      b. Give the disciples a mindset to help each other personally achieve victory.

12. **With The Blessing Of Giving Comes Persecution.** (Mark 10:29-30)
    a. Stay gritty. You will be rewarded for all that you lose for God.

Study 12
Restoration Skills

1. **God Does Not Give Up On Anyone.** (Luke 15:11-32)
    a. Do you know that God is running to welcome a fallaway home? (Luke 15:20)
    b. Have the same attitude about restorations as God the Father, who was looking for the wayward son *"while he was still a long ways off."*
    c. Go through your fallaway membership list every three months to invite those who have fallen away to church.

2. **Preventing Fallaways Is Vital.** (Hebrews 2:1-4)
    a. We must know the elementary teachings and constantly be moving to maturity as this prevents people from drifting and then falling away.

3. **There Are Two Kinds Of Restorations.** (Ezekiel 36:26)
    a. The first kind of restoration is the prodigal son who completely goes into the world. (Luke 15:11-24)
    b. The second kind of restoration are those who *"forsake their first love."* (Revelation 2:4-5) This kind of restoration is usually the case when a remnant person "joins" the SoldOut Movement.
    c. Everyone who is restored must come back to God with all their heart. (2 Corinthians 13:11)

4. **Restored Disciples Are Evangelistic Disciples - Mature Is Fruitful.** (Job 33:26-27)
   a. When someone is in the restoration process, they are often seeking relief from the consequences of sin. However, they need to become fishers of men as part of their restoration, share their faith, and be in Bible studies.

5. **Godly Sorrow Versus Worldly Sorrow.** (2 Corinthians 7:8-11)
   a. Worldy sorrow can be mistaken for Godly sorrow because there are tears.
   b. Godly sorrow is always accompanied by *"earnestness... eagerness, indignation, and alarm."*

6. **It Is Much Harder On The Heart To Be In Sin Than To Be Righteous.** (Matthew 11:28-30)
   a. The yoke of guilt is heavy but working yoked with Jesus is light.

7. **No One Is Too Far Gone.** (2 Chronicles 33:1-17)
   a. Help the person being restored to understand that their best days can be ahead of them.
   b. As a person is being restored, often it is motivating to reestablish "Kingdom dreams." (Haggai 2:9)
   c. God can graft anyone back into the true vine. (Romans 11:22-23)

8. **Restoration Is About Loving Jesus And The Church.** (John 21:15-23)
   a. Jesus called him Simon; his pre-disciple identity had clearly taken over.

b. Jesus expected Peter to shepherd the flock. Peter preached boldly after his restoration on the Day of Pentecost.
   c. Call every restoration back to their *"first love."* (Revelation 2:1-7)

9. **Restored Disciples Restore Others.** (Psalm 51:10-13)
   a. Who do they want to restore? Do they have a list? (Luke 22:31-32)

10. **Restoration Is About Spiritual Openness.** (James 5:16, Proverbs 28:13)
    a. Confession is more than listing off mistakes. It is an acknowledgment that we have sinned against God. (2 Samuel 12:13)

11. **Before You Consider Someone A Fallaway, Be Sure They Are Not Just Really Weak.** (Isaiah 42:3)
    a. If there is a sign of spiritual life, do not consider them dead by taking them off the membership list. If they hear that they were taken off the membership list, that action might be what causes them to really fall away. (Luke 17:1-2)
    b. Restoration is humbling but should not be humiliating. (Galatians 6:1)

12. **God Wants Everyone To Make It.** (2 Peter 3:8-9)
    a. Teach that God is patient and wants us to repent and get back up. (Proverbs 24:16)
    b. Celebrate when the person is restored.

Epilogue
(Do Not Skip)

So Christ Himself gave the apostles, the prophets, the evangelists, the pastors and teachers, to equip His people for works of service, so that the body of Christ may be built up until we all reach unity in the faith and in the knowledge of the Son of God and become mature, attaining to the whole measure of the fullness of Christ.

Then we will no longer be infants, tossed back and forth by the waves, and blown here and there by every wind of teaching and by the cunning and craftiness of people in their deceitful scheming. Instead, speaking the truth in love, we will grow to become in every respect the mature body of Him who is the head, that is, Christ. From Him the whole body, joined and held together by every supporting ligament, grows and builds itself up in love, as each part does its work.
(Ephesians 4:11-16)

Congratulations on completing the *Dodeka Series!* Ideally, these studies were taught in a d-time or a group setting. Prayerfully, you have learned much from the Scriptures and have had many fruitful discussions drawing you closer together with one another and with God. In most cases, if someone has taken the time to do these studies with you, you are part of their Dodeka. However, it is now time for you to raise up your own Dodeka, if you have not already.

As disciples and leaders, we need to be great examples of prayer, devotional life, discipling relationships, and daily personal evangelism. We build our ministries, our schedules, and our priorities around this. (Acts 6:4) We must be able to study the Bible with people and convert them to true Christianity with skill and love. We must be able to count the cost with people to truly "make" amazing disciples in our ministry. We must build an evangelistic heart, culture, and way of life into our ministry!

As leaders, we wake up in the morning, pray and then grab our Bibles and prepare to apply it to ourselves, to make leaders of the disciples around us, and to make disciples out of the non-Christians that we come across. We use the Bible to "level up" everyone we contact all day until we put our heads on the pillow. We are an indomitable force of making the lost into disciples and making disciples into leaders.

After completing this study, it is strongly recommended to study the Book of Acts thoroughly. Take time to write out three or four memorable events from each chapter and memorize them. While *Dodeka* is an effort to teach ministry basics, the Book of Acts shows us how they all fit into God's plan.

Consider, if one goes to a boxing academy and learns the jab, cross punch, hook, uppercut, slip and roll, and practice these in front of a mirror, that does not get them ready for a boxing match. One must watch professional boxers battle and spar themselves. Then one will understand how the moves fit into the greater fight. They will then understand how to add speed, power, heart, urgency, blood, sweat, and tears to win. They will gain the ingenuity to create surprises for one's opponent and build the confidence to take hits and keep going. It takes imitation and then the guts to get into the arena to become a formidable warrior.

There are no extra points for mere knowledge - only impact and effect. (1 Corinthians 8:1) You are now a ministry practitioner. Today, you are called to take all the "moves" you have learned here - continually trying to understand them within the context of the Book of Acts - and implement them with vigor, love, and determination in the fight to win souls.

Today God calls you to be the "tip of the spear" of forceful advancement in His Kingdom! You will give the church the traction that every ministry within so desperately needs. It is time to gird ourselves for action, for we are at the "cutting edge" of Jesus' mission, and I know we will please Him.

In His cause,
Tim Kernan

Made in the USA
Coppell, TX
09 September 2021